A+ Alphabet Books

Pets ABC

An Alphabet Book

by Michael Dahl

Consulting Editor: Gail Saunders-Smith, PhD

Capstone press

Mankato, Minnesota

A is for ant farm.

An ant farm lets you see the tunnels ants dig under the ground. Ants rest in some tunnels and store food in others.

B is for betta fish.

Betta fish are fighting fish. If two male bettas see each other, watch out! They'll bite and thrash and whip their tails.

C is for cage.

A pet bird has flown away.
The cage door was left open.
A cage is a safe place for a pet
when the door stays shut.

D is for dog.

Dogs are friendly and loyal.
But sometimes they find trouble
to get into.

E is for eat.

Pets eat every day. They munch, chomp, and chew. Some pets have little meals. Other pets eat big piles of food.

6

F is for ferret.

Ferrets sometimes are afraid. Bigger pets, such as cats and dogs, might scare a little ferret. Hold a furry ferret, and it will feel safe.

G is for goldfish.

Goldfish gleam and glitter. Their soft fins catch the light. These pets swim round and round in their fishbowls, sparkling like small pieces of gold.

H is for hermit crab.

Hermit crabs hide in empty seashells.
When a hermit crab grows too large
for one shell, it moves to a bigger shell.

I is for iguana.

Iguanas are alert. Their eyes are always open. But when you pet an iguana, its eyes will close. The iguana will relax.

J is for jungle carpet python.

A jungle carpet python's scales form patterns. In the rain forest, the python is hard to see. Its scales blend in with leaves on the rain forest floor.

K is for kitten.

Kittens like soft, small places. They hide in paper bags. Kittens curl up on pillows. A kitten will even hide inside your jacket.

L is for bearded lizard.

A bearded lizard has a flap of skin under its throat. When the lizard is angry or afraid, this floppy beard puffs up like a balloon.

M is for mouse.

A mouse has pink paws and toes.
Its paws are good for grabbing
little things. Its tiny toes are good
for holding on tight.

N is for newt.

The newt stares and stares. Its big eyes blink and look for food. Newts hunt for flies and mosquitoes. A newt will only try to catch food that moves.

O is for owner.

Owners take care of their pets.
They give their pets food and water.
Owners name their pets and talk
to them.

P is for potbellied pig.

This potbellied pig is waiting to play. Its owner taught it a game, and now it wants to play again. Potbellied pigs learn things quickly.

Q is for quaker parrot.

If a quaker parrot cannot see its owner, it thinks the owner is lost. The parrot makes lots of noise to guide the owner safely home. **SQUAWK!**

R is for rabbit.

A rabbit twitches its furry nose. It smells fruits and vegetables. A garden smells like a feast to a hungry rabbit.

S is for snake.

Touch a snake's skin. The skin looks wet and slimy, but a snake feels warm and dry.

T is for turtle.

Turtles are not noisy. Turtles do not run through the house. Turtles do not break things. Turtles are quiet pets.

U is for umbrella cockatoo.

The umbrella cockatoo's beak is strong. This bird comes from the rain forest where there are lots of trees. Cockatoos like to chew on wood and other things.

V is for veterinarian.

Veterinarians look closely at pets' bodies.
They look at pets' eyes, ears, and tongues.
Vets help pets stay healthy and strong.

W is for water dish.

The water dish was full of water. Now it is empty. Someone's pet was thirsty. **SLURP. SLURP.**

X is for exercise.

Many pets need exercise. They need to run and play. After all its exercise, this mouse is still in the same place.

Y is for yellow tang.

The yellow tang has a long yellow mouth.
This fish's mouth can reach deep into
rocky cracks to bite tasty plants.

Z is for zebra finch.

Zebra finches are never alone. They sit together, and they sing together. They also sleep together. **ZZZZZ.**

Fun Facts about Pets

According to a recent survey, the most popular name for a dog is Max. Other popular names include Molly, Sam, Zach, and Maggie.

Goldfish lose their color if they are kept in dim light or placed in a body of running water, such as a stream.

A snake uses its tongue to smell. Snakes stick out their tongues to pick up scents.

In Egypt 4,000 years ago, the penalty for killing a cat was death.

Cats, not dogs, are the most common pets in the United States. There are about 66 million cats and 58 million dogs. Parakeets are third at 14 million.

Pet parrots can learn to copy sounds, such as words and whistles. Wild parrots may copy sounds, but they don't learn to say words.

Research has proven that people who own pets live longer, have less stress, and suffer fewer heart attacks.

Glossary

alert (uh-LURT)—paying attention

exercise (EK-sur-size)—a physical activity done in order to stay healthy and fit

pattern (PAT-urn)—a repeating arrangement of colors and shapes

rain forest (RAYN FOR-ist)—a thick forest where a great deal of rain falls

tunnel (TUHN-uhl)—an underground passage

twitch (TWICH)—to make small, jerky movements

veterinarian (vet-ur-uh-NER-ee-uhn)—a doctor who treats sick or injured animals; veterinarians help animals stay healthy.

Read More

Gogerly, Liz. *Pets.* Starters. North Mankato, Minn.: Smart Apple Media, 2004.

Goldsack, Gabby. *Pets.* Busy Books. Columbus, Ohio: Waterbird Books, 2004.

Stanley, Mandy. *Perfect Pets.* All Aboard. New York: Kingfisher, 2004.

Internet Sites

FactHound offers a safe, fun way to find Internet sites related to this book. All of the sites on FactHound have been researched by our staff.

Here's how:
1. Visit *www.facthound.com*
2. Type in this special code **0736826076** for age-appropriate sites. Or enter a search word related to this book for a more general search.
3. Click on the **Fetch It** button.

FactHound will fetch the best sites for you!

Index

A+ Books are published by Capstone Press
151 Good Counsel Drive, P.O. Box 669, Mankato, Minnesota 56002
www.capstonepress.com

1 2 3 4 5 6 09 08 07 06 05 04

Library of Congress Cataloging-in-Publication Data
Dahl, Michael.
    Pets ABC: an alphabet book / by Michael Dahl.
    p. cm.— (A+ alphabet books)
    Includes bibliographical references (p. 31) and index.
    ISBN 0-7368-2607-6 (hardcover)
    1. Pets—Juvenile literature. 2. English language—Alphabet—Juvenile literature. I. Title.
SF416.2.D34 2004
428.1'3—dc22   2004001042

Summary: Introduces pets through photographs and brief text that uses one word relating to
    pets for each letter of the alphabet.

Credits
Blake Hoena and June Preszler, editors; Heather Kindseth, designer; Kelly Garvin,
    photo researcher; Eric Kudalis, product planning editor

Photo Credits
Brand X Pictures/Alley Cat Productions, 5, 6, 8, 25; Bruce Coleman Inc., 9; Bruce Coleman Inc./Ernest Janes, 27; Bruce Coleman Inc./Gail M. Shumway, 3; Bruce Coleman Inc./Jane Burton, 12; Bruce Coleman Inc./Lee Rentz, 15; Capstone Press/Gary Sundermeyer, 11, 18; Corbis/Ariel Skelley, 20; Corbis/Chris Collins, 14; Corbis/Jon Feingersh, 21; Corbis/Jose Luis Pelaez Inc., 4; Corbis/LWA-Dann Tardif, cover; Corbis/LWA-JDC, 23; Corbis/Paul Barton, 16; Corbis/RF, 24; Corbis/Thom Lang, 2; Creatas, 26; PhotoDisc Inc., 28 (both), 29 (right); PhotoDisc Inc./G.K. & Vikki Hart, 1, 13, 29 (left); Ron Kimball Stock/Ron Kimball, 7, 10, 17, 19, 22

Note to Parents, Teachers, and Librarians
Pets ABC: An Alphabet Book uses colorful photographs and a nonfiction format to introduce children to pets while building a mastery of the alphabet. This book is designed to be read independently by an early reader or to be read aloud to a pre-reader. The images help early readers and listeners understand the text and concepts discussed. The book encourages further learning by including the following sections: Fun Facts about Pets, Glossary, Read More, Internet Sites, and Index. Early readers may need assistance using these features.